THE BOOK OF Hosea

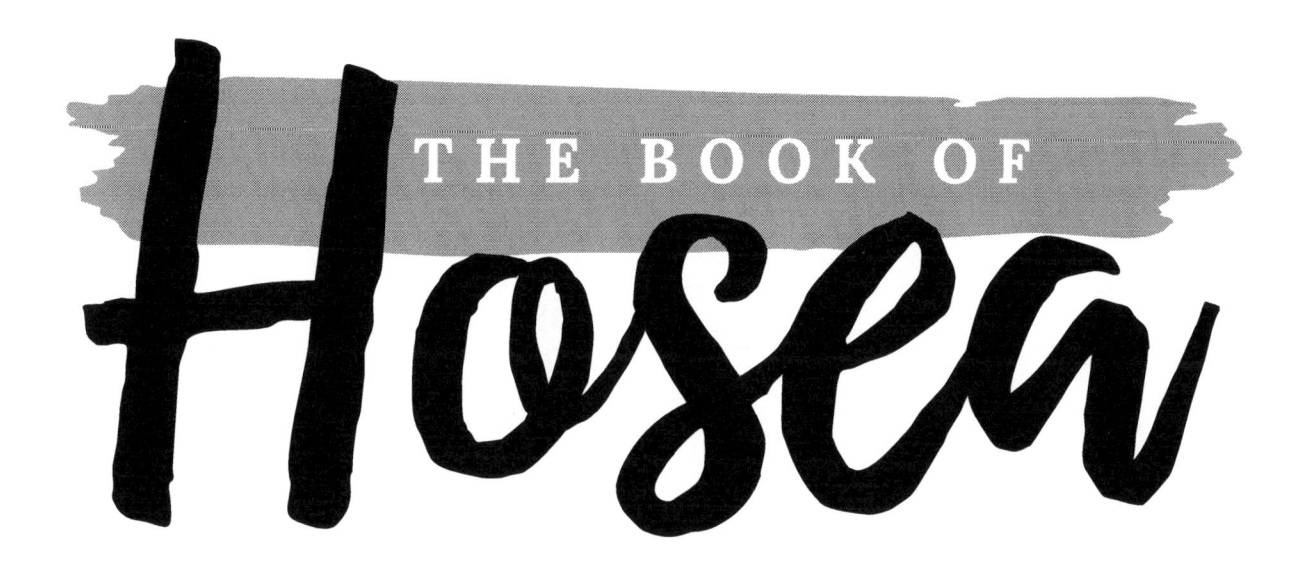

ONE CHAPTER A DAY

GoodMorningGirls.org

The Book of Hosea

© 2020 Women Living Well Ministries, LLC

ALL RIGHTS RESERVED

No part of this book may be reproduced in any form or by any electronic or mechanical means, including information storage and retrieval systems, without written permission from the author, except in the case of a reviewer, who may quote brief passages embodied in critical articles or in a review.

Scripture is from the ESV® Bible (The Holy Bible, English Standard Version®), copyright © 2001 by Crossway Bibles, a publishing ministry of Good News Publishers. Used by permission. All rights reserved.

Welcome to Good Morning Girls! We are so glad you are joining us.

God created us to walk with Him, to know Him, and to be loved by Him. He is our living well, and when we drink from the water He continually provides, His living water will change the entire course of our lives.

> *Jesus said: "Whoever drinks of the water that I will give him will never be thirsty again. The water that I will give him will become in him a spring of water welling up to eternal life." ~ John 4:14 (ESV)*

So let's begin.

The method we use here at GMG is called the **SOAK** method.

- ❏ **S**—The S stands for *Scripture*—Read the chapter for the day. Then choose 1-2 verses and write them out word for word. (There is no right or wrong choice—just let the Holy Spirit guide you.)

- ❏ **O**—The O stands for *Observation*—Look at the verse or verses you wrote out. Write 1 or 2 observations. What stands out to you? What do you learn about the character of God from these verses? Is there a promise, command or teaching?

- ❏ **A**—The A stands for *Application*—Personalize the verses. What is God saying to you? How can you apply them to your life? Are there any changes you need to make or an action to take?

- ❏ **K**—The K stands for *Kneeling in Prayer*—Pause, kneel and pray. Confess any sin God has revealed to you today. Praise God for His word. Pray the passage over your own life or someone you love. Ask God to help you live out your applications.

SOAK God's word into your heart and squeeze every bit of nourishment you can out of each day's scripture reading. Soon you will find your life transformed by the renewing of your mind!

Walk with the King!

Courtney

WomenLivingWell.org, GoodMorningGirls.org

Join the GMG Community

Share your daily SOAK on **Facebook.com/GoodMorningGirlsWLW**

Instagram: **WomenLivingWell #WomenLivingWell**

GMG Bible Coloring Chart

COLORS	KEYWORDS
PURPLE	God, Jesus, Holy Spirit, Saviour, Messiah
PINK	women of the Bible, family, marriage, parenting, friendship, relationships
RED	love, kindness, mercy, compassion, peace, grace
GREEN	faith, obedience, growth, fruit, salvation, fellowship, repentance
YELLOW	worship, prayer, praise, doctrine, angels, miracles, power of God, blessings
BLUE	wisdom, teaching, instruction, commands
ORANGE	prophecy, history, times, places, kings, genealogies, people, numbers, covenants, vows, visions, oaths, future
BROWN/GRAY	Satan, sin, death, hell, evil, idols, false teachers, hypocrisy, temptation

Introduction to the Book of Hosea

The book of Hosea is a picture of God's great love for his people. Though Israel was unfaithful to God, God still loved them but Israel's failure to heed the prophetic warnings of Hosea and continue in their idolatry and disobedience to God, led to consequences.

Israel reaped what they had sown because of their refusal to repent. But even in God's judgement of them, God demonstrated his compassion and love for them in leaving them a remnant, that would be restored to him.

The Book of Hosea has two parts. The first three chapters use Hosea's life to illustrate his prophetic message, as he marries Gomer, who is repeatedly unfaithful to him. Hosea continues to love his wife, despite her unfaithfulness to him. His marriage was a picture of God's covenantal love for his people and Israel's continual unfaithfulness to Him.

The last eleven chapters of Hosea record the accusations against Israel and the warnings for them to turn and repent of their disobedient ways. These chapters reveal the character and heart of God, as he is torn by his love and compassion for them and their need for discipline. In the end, they face judgement but there is hope as God's healing love is poured out on them.

The Purpose: Though the book of Hosea focuses on the judgement of Israel, it more deeply represents God's deep and enduring love for his people. Despite Israel running after other gods and living as if they were not God's people, God desired to restore his relationship with them. So God went after them, to bring them back to himself.

The Author: Hosea was a minor prophet, who prophesied during the last 40 years of the Northern Kingdom.

Time Period: This book was written between 790 and 710 B.C. Hosea prophesied at the same time as Amos, Isaiah and Micah, during the time period of 2nd Kings 15.

Key Verse: Hosea 6:6: *"For I desire steadfast love and not sacrifice, the knowledge of God rather than burnt offerings."*

The Outline:

Hosea's Family

1. Hosea marries Gomer. (1)

2. Israel is unfaithful. (2)

3. Hosea redeems and reconciles with his wife. (3)

Israel Commits Spiritual Adultery

    4. The Lord's case against Israel. (4)

    5. God's judgement against Judah and Israel. (5)

    6. A call to repentance. (6)

Israel Refuses to Repent

    7. Israel is unrepentant. (7)

    8. An announcement of judgement. (8)

    9. Israel's captivity. (9)

    10. The Lord punishes Israel. (10)

God's Love for Israel

    11. God loves rebellious Israel. (11)

    12. The indictment of Israel and Judah. (12)

    13. God's anger and judgement of Israel. (13)

    14. A call to return to the Lord for restoration. (14)

As we study the book of Hosea together, we will see how applicable this book is to our own lives. The same God that loved and pursued Israel, loves and pursues us. God loves us so much, he sent his son Jesus to die on the cross, so that we could be forgiven of our sins and saved from judgement.

You are dearly loved by your heavenly Father and He desires a close relationship with you. No matter what you have done or how much you have sinned, when you repent, God is faithful to forgive. He loves you so much!

So, let's get started studying God's word! Be sure to set aside at least 15 minutes a day, for your reading. I can't wait to see how God reveals himself personally to each of us, as we read the book of Hosea together, chapter by chapter.

Keep walking with the King!

Courtney

The word of the Lord

that came to Hosea...

Hosea 1:1

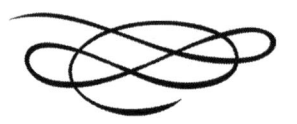

Reflection Question:

The word of the Lord came to Hosea, but the word was not for Israel. First, it was for Hosea. God asked Hosea to marry Gomer, as a picture of the unfaithfulness of Israel. Hosea would experience the feelings that God feels, when his people are unfaithful to him.

Sometimes when we read God's word, it is tempting to apply it first to others. But we must always remember to apply God's word first to our own lives, before we teach it to others. Hosea prophesied to Israel out of his own suffering and life experience. How have you experienced God in your own life and how can you use that to minister to others?

Hosea 1

S—The S stands for *Scripture*

O—The O stands for *Observation*

A—The A stands for *Application*

K—The K stands for *Kneeling in Prayer*

I will betroth you to me forever.

Hosea 2:19

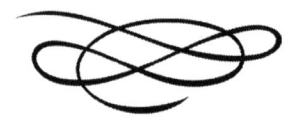

Reflection Question:

Israel's relationship with God was broken because of their unfaithfulness to him. They sought after the passing pleasure of sin, over the blessings of God and so God said they would be disciplined. After their discipline was complete, God said he would speak tender words to them, to draw them back and restore them to himself forever.

After we fall into sin, God's heart is always that his people would be restored to him. Think of a time when you have been tempted to go off the path that God has for you? What drew you away? How did God bring you back? Was it through discipline or tender words? How is your relationship with God deeper as a result of his mercy and grace?

Hosea 2

S—The S stands for *Scripture*

O—The O stands for *Observation*

A—The A stands for *Application*

K—The K stands for *Kneeling in Prayer*

> *"Go again, love a woman who is loved by another man and is an adulteress, even as the Lord loves the children of Israel, though they turn to other gods."*
>
> Hosea 3:1

Reflection Question:

God commanded Hosea to go and love his adulteress wife. Hosea's love was to be an illustration of God's love for his people, who were spiritual adulterers. God still loved his people, despite how they had turned to other gods.

God's love, compassion and forgiveness towards us is greater than we can ever imagine. How does knowing God's great love for you, even when you fail, challenge you to love and forgive others in your life?

Hosea 3

S—The S stands for *Scripture*

O—The O stands for *Observation*

A—The A stands for *Application*

K—The K stands for *Kneeling in Prayer*

My people are destroyed

for lack of knowledge

Hosea 4:6

Reflection Question:

The Lord brings an accusation against Israel that they have no faithfulness, no steadfast love and no knowledge of God in the land. As a result, they have no restraint. They are swearing, lying, murdering, stealing, committing adultery and self-destructing.

God's people were being destroyed for their lack of knowledge and rejection of knowledge. They had forgotten the law of the Lord and their sin was increasing. When you miss your daily time in God's Word, how does it affect you and your daily choices? How does seeing the rejection of knowledge by God's people, remind you of the importance of being in God's word every day?

Hosea 4

S—The S stands for **Scripture**

O—The O stands for **Observation**

A—The A stands for **Application**

K—The K stands for **Kneeling in Prayer**

I will return again to my place,

until they acknowledge their guilt

and seek my face,

and in their distress earnestly seek me.

Hosea 5:15

Reflection Question:

Naaman, a mighty man of valor, was at the top of his game but he was dying of leprosy. A brave little girl from Israel told him about the prophet Elisha. If she had been wrong, she would have been in danger, but she was right. Elisha sent word that Naaman should wash in the Jordan seven times to be healed but this did not meet Naaman's expectations. It angered him. He expected Elisha to come to him and cure him. Instead, it required Naaman to act in faith and do it himself. Naaman was healed without Elisha being nearby and as a result, God received all the glory.

Elisha repeatedly asked those who were seeking the Lord's help to take part in their miracles. It required faith from those who sought the Lord. As a result, God received all the praise, rather than Elisha. Elisha's instructions were simple yet very difficult for a prideful man. Naaman had to overcome his pride in order to receive from the Lord. Reflect on your own life. In what area do you struggle with pride especially when it comes to following the Lord? And in what area are you leaning too hard on another person, rather than on God?

Hosea 5

S—The S stands for **Scripture**

O—The O stands for **Observation**

A—The A stands for **Application**

K—The K stands for **Kneeling in Prayer**

For I desire steadfast love and not sacrifice.

Hosea 6:6

Reflection Question:

Hosea led the people in a prayer of repentance. Hosea understood God's loving discipline was meant to heal them rather than strike them down. He had full confidence that God would restore them, but Israel and Judah's love was temporary, like a morning cloud. They were willing to make sacrifices to God, but they did not have a steadfast love for God and so they sinned in their unfaithfulness.

Hosea 6:6 says: "For I desire steadfast love and not sacrifice." Jesus quoted Hosea 6:6 in Matthew 9:13 and Matthew 12:7. God delights more in our deep love for him, than the following of rituals. Sometimes we may be tempted to check certain boxes that show we love God, like going to church and putting money in the offering plate, but God wants a close relationship with us. In what ways are you tempted to be busy serving God, while missing out on just being still with God in prayer and the reading of his word? How can you offer God more steadfast love and not just sacrifice?

Hosea 6

S—The S stands for *Scripture*

O—The O stands for *Observation*

A—The A stands for *Application*

K—The K stands for *Kneeling in Prayer*

Woe to them,

for they have strayed from me

Hosea 7:13

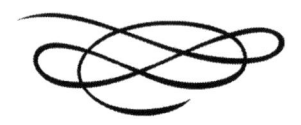

Reflection Question:

Israel's sins were before the face of God, but they did not consider that with God, there are no secrets. Like an oven, blazing with fire, Israel was inflamed with passions and desires for other gods and their pride blinded them and so they strayed and rebelled against God. They cried over their problems, but they did not consider that they should repent of their sin, which was the cause of their problems.

Our greatest love and affection should be for God but sometimes our fleshly passions and desires lead us astray. Are you struggling with a secret sin right now? Have you considered that God sees and knows your struggles and if you do not confess your sin, it could lead to trouble in the future? Pray now and ask the Lord to help you overcome any desires that compete with your love and affection for God.

Hosea 7

S—The S stands for *Scripture*

O—The O stands for *Observation*

A—The A stands for *Application*

K—The K stands for *Kneeling in Prayer*

For they sow the wind,

and they shall reap the whirlwind.

Hosea 8:7

Reflection Question:

As God pronounced the judgement, about to come on Israel, the people cried out, "My God, we know you." Many church goers might say this on judgement day. But Israel had rejected God and followed idols. Now they were about to reap what they had sown, over a long period of time. And though the sowing was slow, the reaping would be sudden like a whirlwind.

Divine discipline follows the law of sowing and reaping. If we sow bad decisions in our lives, we will suffer. Sometimes we might be tempted to think we can get away with doing wrong, but God always sees and knows. We are responsible to choose right over wrong, even when it requires time and patience. It is worth the effort in the long run. Is there an area in your life right now, where you are compromising?

Hosea 8

S—The S stands for *Scripture*

O—The O stands for *Observation*

A—The A stands for *Application*

K—The K stands for *Kneeling in Prayer*

My God will reject them because they have not listened to him.

Hosea 9:17

Reflection Question:

Israel had grown accustomed to plentiful harvests and blessings but due to their disobedience, their crops were about to fail. They would be taken into exile, where they would mourn and have bread only for survival. God remembers a time when Israel was fruitful, but they had now become detestable like the gods they served. And so, there would be no more fruitfulness in the land, but rather barrenness because they had not listened to God.

Because of the people's deep corruption, they called Hosea a fool (9:7). They were experiencing great blessing and pleasure and so they could not imagine the coming judgement that Hosea foretold. But Hosea continued to boldly prophecy. Are you afraid to share the gospel because of what people will think or say about you? How does Hosea's bravery encourage you?

Hosea 9

S—The S stands for *Scripture*

O—The O stands for *Observation*

A—The A stands for *Application*

K—The K stands for *Kneeling in Prayer*

> *Sow for yourselves righteousness;*
>
> *reap steadfast love;*
>
> *break up your fallow ground,*
>
> *for it is the time to seek the Lord.*
>
> Hosea 10:12

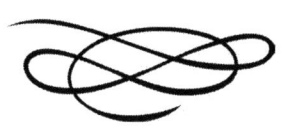

Reflection Question:

Israel used their blessings in ungodly ways, but even in their sin, if they would turn back and sow righteousness, steadfast love and seek the Lord, God would bless them. But instead they continued to trust in their own way and harden their hearts.

Once again, we see the law of sowing and reaping in the book of Hosea. The hearts of Israel were hard and needed broken, so they could sow seeds of righteousness. If they would seek the Lord, he would bless them, and they would be fruitful again. Isn't the availability of God's grace so encouraging? Even though we may go astray, if we will turn from our ways and once again seek to sow seeds of righteousness, God will honor that. All sin starts when we trust our own ways rather than God's. In what area of your life do you need to trust God more and sow more seeds of righteousness?

Hosea 10

S—The S stands for **Scripture**

O—The O stands for **Observation**

A—The A stands for **Application**

K—The K stands for **Kneeling in Prayer**

> *For I am God and not a man,*
> *the Holy One in your midst.*
>
> *Hosea 11:9*

Reflection Question:

God's tender and parental love for Israel is seen as he speaks of his fond memories of them from the past. God won Israel's heart with his love rather than by force and He served them by meeting their needs and giving them rest. It was not their sin that was bringing discipline but rather their refusal to repent of their sin, that was leading to discipline. But God took no pleasure in knowing that they would face judgement. He promised to leave a remnant to restore them because of his deep love for them.

God's love is not like man's love. God is holy and perfect. His patience, compassion, kindness and forgiveness are beyond what any man can give. And though God is not man, because of his great love for us, he came as a man, to die on the cross for our sins. Pause for a moment and consider how deeply loved you are by God. Even when you mess up and make wrong choices, when you repent, you are forgiven and unconditionally loved because you are his child. How does remembering how loved you are by God, draw you towards him in obedience? Give thanks to God for his loving kindness right now and tell him how much you love him.

Hosea 11

S—The S stands for *Scripture*

O—The O stands for *Observation*

A—The A stands for *Application*

K—The K stands for *Kneeling in Prayer*

Hold fast to love and justice,

and wait continually for your God.

Hosea 12:6

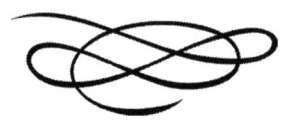

Reflection Question:

Despite being warned over and over, Israel continued their empty pursuits. So, God reminded Israel of their father Jacob and how he wrestled with God, refusing to submit to him. In the end, Jacob wept desperately as he sought God's blessing. But even Jacob had to flee from his homeland, when he ran from Esau and Jacob ended up in exile, just as Israel would.

God initiated a wrestling match with Jacob because he needed Jacob's full attention and submission, in order to bless him. I'm sure the last thing Jacob felt like he needed was a wrestling match with God, but God knew what he needed. When Jacob finally came to the end of himself, that is when he received the blessing. What are you wrestling with today? Go to God in prayer and do not give up. Stay with God until he drives out all of your fear and anxiety because when you are done wrestling with God, you will find a peace and blessing that you would not have without it. Remember that the way God answers your prayer may not be what you desire but God will show up and he will do what is best for you and for his glory.

Hosea 12

S—The S stands for *Scripture*

O—The O stands for *Observation*

A—The A stands for *Application*

K—The K stands for *Kneeling in Prayer*

You know no God but me,

and besides me there is no savior.

Hosea 13:4

Reflection Question:

Israel continued to sin more and more but like the morning dew, they would not be able to stand up under God's judgement. The only one who could save them was God, who they had rejected. They rejected God as their king and begged for other kings, who could not save them. But times were good, so they forgot about God but now, judgement was about to be as intense as pangs of childbirth. It would be sudden and unexpectedly, as they bore the guilt of their sin, until they turned back to God.

Even though Israel had put their trust in other gods and in their own strength, God continued to protect them and care for them. When times are good and we are experiencing God's protection and care, we can be tempted to forget God. But there is no other God but our God and no other savior but our savior. In what ways are you tempted to trust in your own strength rather than in God's care for you? And how does seeing Israel forget God in the good times, remind you to not forget God in your good times?

Hosea 13

S—The S stands for **Scripture**

O—The O stands for **Observation**

A—The A stands for **Application**

K—The K stands for **Kneeling in Prayer**

Whoever is wise, let him understand these things;

whoever is discerning, let him know them;

for the ways of the Lord are right,

and the upright walk in them.

Hosea 14:9

Reflection Question:

This chapter in Hosea is one of the most beautiful chapters in the Old Testament. It reveals the loving heart of God, as his people experience his mercy, love, blessing and complete restoration after a time of judgement. He compares them to the beauty of a lily, the strength of roots of a tree, the value of the olive, and the delightful fragrance of Lebanon. The fame of Israel is restored as God promises to look after them and be like an evergreen cypress, providing fruitfulness to them.

Oh, what a loving and gracious God we serve! Our God is full of compassion and he loves you deeply. No sin is beyond his forgiveness. He is forever faithful to us. The final words of Hosea 14 tell us, that those who are wise, understand these things and whoever is discerning, knows them. For the ways of the Lord are right and the upright walk in them. How does this challenge you to carefully follow God's Word? What is one new thing you learned during your study in the book of Hosea?

Hosea 14

S—The S stands for *Scripture*

O—The O stands for *Observation*

A—The A stands for *Application*

K—The K stands for *Kneeling in Prayer*

Made in the USA
Columbia, SC
13 July 2025